KT-450-965

RSPB

RSPB first book of
minibeasts

Anita Ganeri and David Chandler

30131 05078781 8

LONDON BOROUGH OF BARNET

Published 2011 by A&C Black,
An Imprint of Bloomsbury Publishing Plc
50 Bedford Square, London WC1B 3DP
www.bloomsbury.com

ISBN: 978-1-4081-3715-4

Copyright © 2011 Bloomsbury Publishing Plc
Text © Anita Ganeri, David Chandler, 2011
Illustrations © Robin Bouttell, 2011

All rights reserved. No part of this publication may
be reproduced in any form or by any means –
photographic, electronic, taping or information
storage and retrieval systems – without the prior
written permission of the publishers.

Printed and bound in China by WKT.

A&C Black uses paper produced from elemental
chlorine-free pulp, harvested from managed
sustainable forests.

10 9 8 7 6 5 4 3 2

MIX
Paper from
responsible sources
FSC www.fsc.org
FSC® C010256

Contents

Minibeasts

Minibeasts are everywhere! They are hopping, buzzing, crawling and wriggling all around you.

This book will help you name lots of the minibeasts you can see. It also tells you about what they do and where they like to live. Watch bees and butterflies visiting flowers. Look under logs or rocks for beetles and woodlice (ask an adult to help). Discover spiders in hedges and bushes or sit by a pond and spot dragonflies and pond skaters.

At the back of this book is a Spotter's Guide to help you remember the minibeasts you spot. You could also write down the minibeasts you see, or draw them.

Turn the page to find out all about minibeasts!

Dragonfly

This is an emperor dragonfly. It is the biggest dragonfly in Britain. It has huge eyes for spotting insects to eat. Look out for it by water on warm summer days.

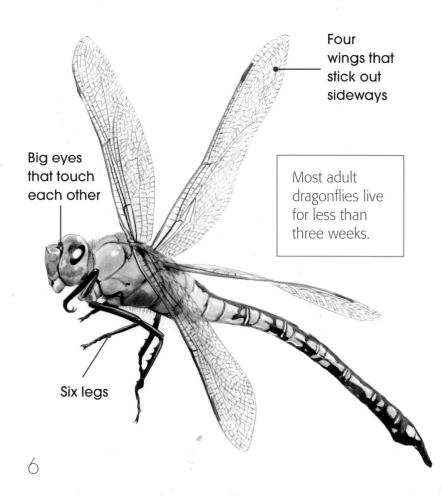

Four wings that stick out sideways

Big eyes that touch each other

Most adult dragonflies live for less than three weeks.

Six legs

Damselfly

A damselfly looks like a small dragonfly. This is a common blue damselfly. It folds its wings over its back when it is resting.

Dragonflies and damselflies spend most of their lives growing up underwater.

Big eyes that don't touch each other

Like dragonflies, damselflies eat insects.

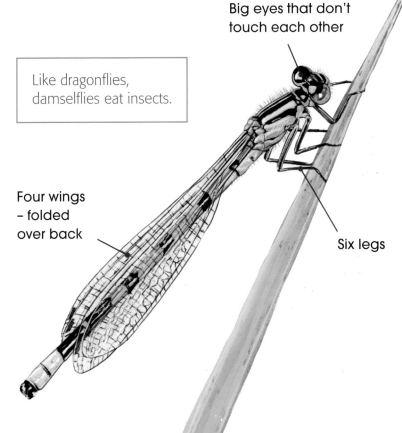

Four wings – folded over back

Six legs

7

Bumblebee

Look for bumblebees in the garden. They buzz around flowers, searching for nectar. Look at their big, hairy bodies. Many have yellow, orange, red or white stripes.

Bumblebees don't sting very often.

Hairy body

Hairy legs

Tongue

A bumblebee's bright colours warn other animals to stay away.

Honeybee

Most honeybees are hairy and brown. They collect nectar from flowers. Then they take this to their hive, where they turn the nectar into honey.

Like bumblebees, honeybees hardly ever sting.

They do a special dance to show other honeybees where the food is.

Stripes

Wasp

The wasps you are most likely to see are common wasps. Most of them will die before winter comes. Only the queen wasps survive.

Common wasps build their nests out of paper, made from chewed-up wood.

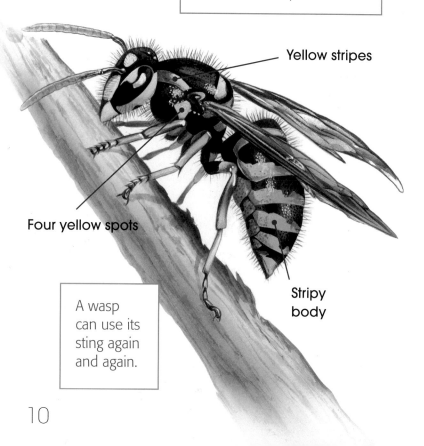

Yellow stripes

Four yellow spots

A wasp can use its sting again and again.

Stripy body

Ant

This is a black garden ant. Lots of ants live together in ant nests. They make their nests in the soil and under stones. They eat sweet foods, like honeydew made by aphids.

Look for swarms of flying ants in the summer. This is when the males and females mate.

You might also see other types of ant. They can be red-brown or yellow.

Strong jaws

Black body

Thin 'waist'

11

Cinnabar moth

These red and black moths fly in the day and the night. Look for them between May and August. You can see them in grassy fields, sand dunes, gardens and woods.

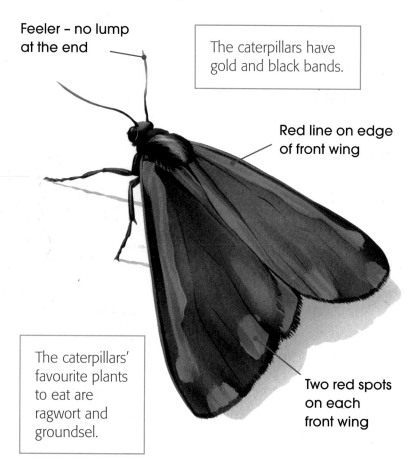

Feeler – no lump at the end

The caterpillars have gold and black bands.

Red line on edge of front wing

The caterpillars' favourite plants to eat are ragwort and groundsel.

Two red spots on each front wing

Garden tiger moth

This colourful moth comes out at night in July and August. On a sunny day you might see a garden tiger caterpillar. It is red-brown and black, and hairy. It is called a 'woolly bear'.

Garden tiger moths all have slightly different patterns on their wings.

Feeler

Brown and white pattern

Their bright colours are a warning. They tell animals not to eat them because they taste horrible!

Orange-red with blue-black spots

Common blue butterfly

Look for common blue butterflies in gardens, meadows and woods. They like warm, sunny places. This is a male. Females have browner wings.

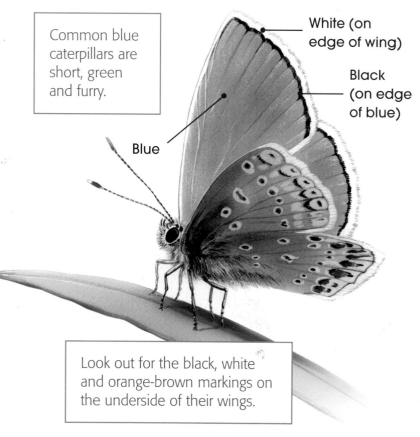

Common blue caterpillars are short, green and furry.

White (on edge of wing)

Black (on edge of blue)

Blue

Look out for the black, white and orange-brown markings on the underside of their wings.

Large white butterfly

A male large white butterfly has big, black tips on its front wings. The female has two black spots on the top of her front wings as well.

Large white caterpillars eat cabbage and brussel sprout plants.

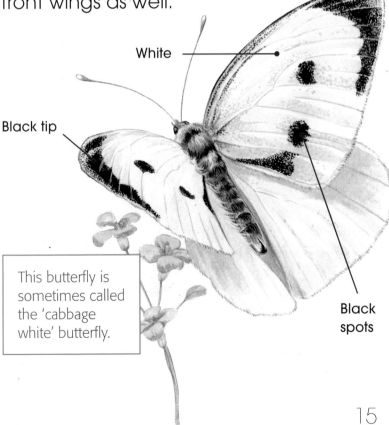

White

Black tip

This butterfly is sometimes called the 'cabbage white' butterfly.

Black spots

Red admiral butterfly

These handsome butterflies are easy to spot. You often see them in gardens. Red admirals feed on nectar and rotting fruit. They lay their eggs on nettle leaves.

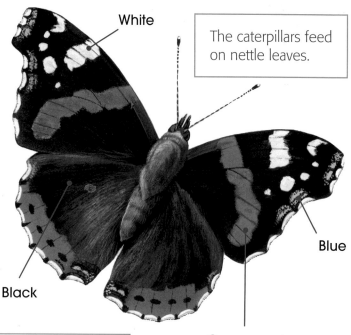

White

The caterpillars feed on nettle leaves.

Blue

Black

Orange-red

Red admirals fly here from other countries.

Brimstone butterfly

A male brimstone butterfly has bright yellow wings. The female is much paler. Brimstone butterflies sleep all winter. Sometimes they wake up as early as February!

Look at the colour of the male brimstone. That's where butterflies get their name!

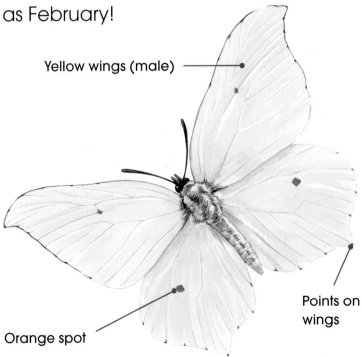

Yellow wings (male)

Points on wings

Orange spot

Pond skater

You can see pond skaters on ponds, lakes and rivers. Look for the dips where their legs touch the surface. Pond skaters eat insects that get stuck on the water.

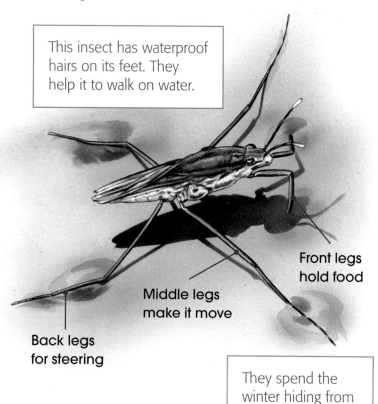

This insect has waterproof hairs on its feet. They help it to walk on water.

Front legs hold food

Middle legs make it move

Back legs for steering

They spend the winter hiding from the cold, a long way from water.

Common backswimmer

You can see these in ponds, lakes and rivers. Don't mix one up with a lesser water boatman. The backswimmer swims on its back. The lesser water boatman swims on its front.

Common backswimmers eat small fish, tadpoles and insects.

Look for them hanging under the water surface.

Long back legs for rowing

Sharp beak

Don't pick one up – it might bite you!

House fly

House flies live where people live. You might see and hear them buzzing around your house. They like to lay their eggs in horse poo and pig poo!

The house fly is one of the most common insects in the world.

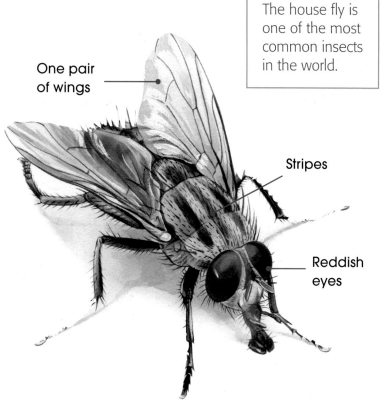

One pair of wings

Stripes

Reddish eyes

Bluebottle

This fly is bigger than a house fly. It is hairy and has a shiny, blue body. If you see a bluebottle in your house, it is probably a female. She is trying to find somewhere to lay her eggs. Most males stay outside and feed on nectar.

Bluebottles eat things that are dead or nearly dead.

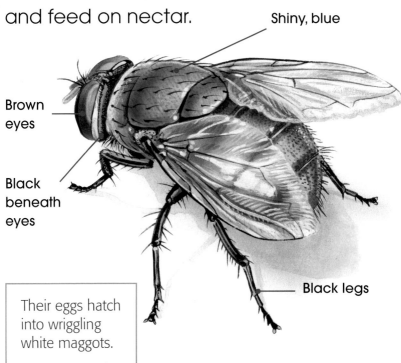

Shiny, blue

Brown eyes

Black beneath eyes

Black legs

Their eggs hatch into wriggling white maggots.

Cranefly

Lots of people call these 'daddy-long-legs'. They have very long legs and only one pair of wings. Craneflies usually come out at night. You sometimes see them fluttering around lights.

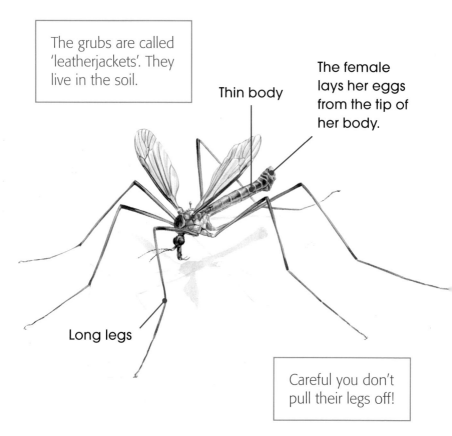

The grubs are called 'leatherjackets'. They live in the soil.

Thin body

The female lays her eggs from the tip of her body.

Long legs

Careful you don't pull their legs off!

Hoverfly

Most hoverflies look like wasps or bees. But, it's a trick – hoverflies cannot sting. Their bright colours trick their enemies into leaving them alone.

Hoverflies live in gardens, parks, woods and meadows.

Many hoverflies feed on nectar.

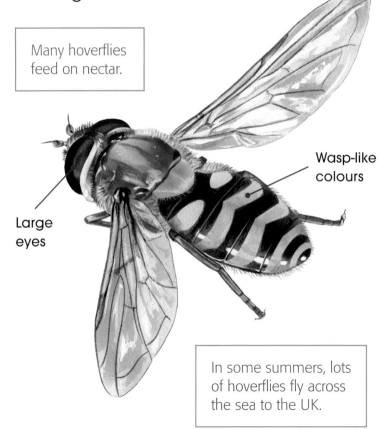

Wasp-like colours

Large eyes

In some summers, lots of hoverflies fly across the sea to the UK.

Earwig

Earwigs are shiny brown. They have pincers at the back end of their bodies. Males fight each other with their pincers. Earwigs come out at night. In the day, they rest under stones and logs.

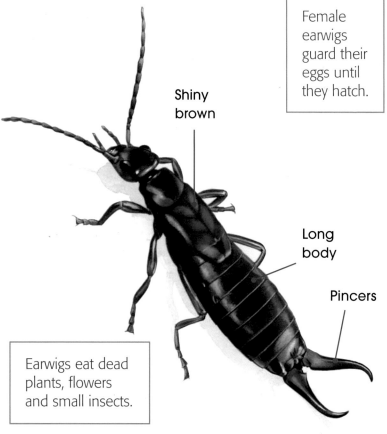

Female earwigs guard their eggs until they hatch.

Shiny brown

Long body

Pincers

Earwigs eat dead plants, flowers and small insects.

Green lacewing

Green lacewings come out at night and are attracted to lights. Look for them after dark on a window that is lit up. They get their name from their lace-like wings.

Lacewing grubs suck the juices out of aphids.

Long feelers

Lace-like wings

Green body

When they spend the winter in a house they change colour to pinkish-brown.

Mosquito

You might hear a mosquito before you see it. It makes a high whining buzz. Females have sharp tubes instead of mouths. The female sticks her tube into animals and feeds on their blood. The male eats nectar and honeydew.

Mosquito grubs are wriggly. Look for them in water.

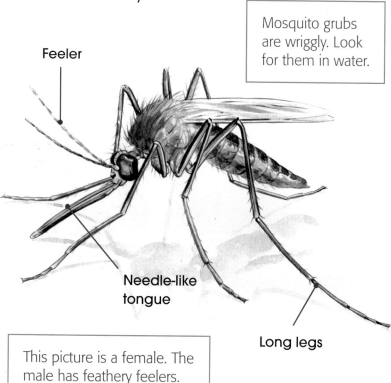

Feeler

Needle-like tongue

Long legs

This picture is a female. The male has feathery feelers.

Common froghopper

You might find one of these insects in your garden. Even though it is so small, it can jump very high! It feeds on juices from plants. Look out for froghoppers between June and October.

Froghopper grubs live inside a ball of froth. It is called 'cuckoo spit'.

Frog-like face

The grubs grow up safely inside the froth then crawl out as adults and hop away.

Green shield bug

A green shield bug is shaped like a shield. In summer, it is bright green like grass. In winter, it turns brown like dead leaves. Its colour helps to hide it from hungry birds and insects.

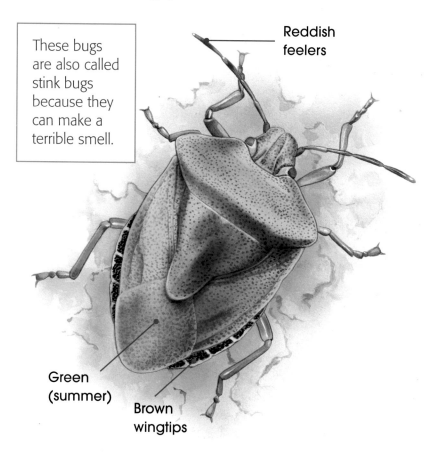

These bugs are also called stink bugs because they can make a terrible smell.

Reddish feelers

Green (summer)

Brown wingtips

Devil's coach-horse

This beetle comes out at night. It hunts other insects, worms, spiders and slugs. It eats dead animals too. To find one in the daytime, look under logs.

Handle with care – they bite!

Pincer-like jaws

Long black body

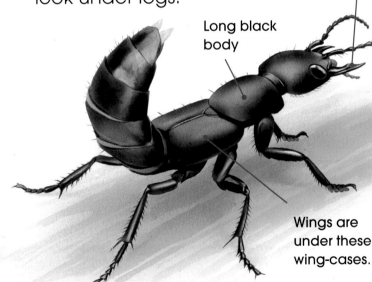

Wings are under these wing-cases.

To defend itself, a devil's coach-horse curls up its tail. It also squirts out a smelly liquid.

Soldier beetle

You can see soldier beetles from May to August. Look for them on the tops of flowers. They might be mating or hunting insects to eat.

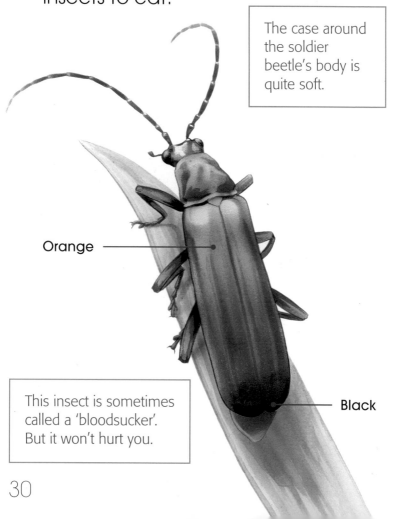

The case around the soldier beetle's body is quite soft.

Orange

This insect is sometimes called a 'bloodsucker'. But it won't hurt you.

Black

Ladybird

This is a seven-spot ladybird. It is easy to see, with its bright red body. Some types of ladybird are yellow and black. Their bright colours warn hungry hunters that they taste horrible.

Ladybirds eat aphids that damage garden plants.

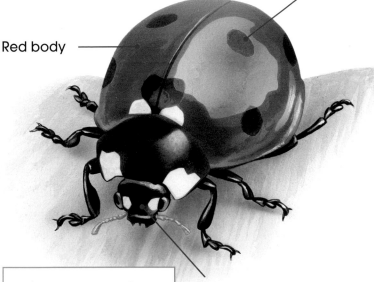

Seven black spots

Red body

Take care – sometimes ladybirds' legs squirt out a smelly liquid.

Black-and-white head

Cockchafer

Cockchafers are big beetles. They come out at night. You can see them from May to August. Look for the fan-shaped feelers on a male. They use them to sniff out females.

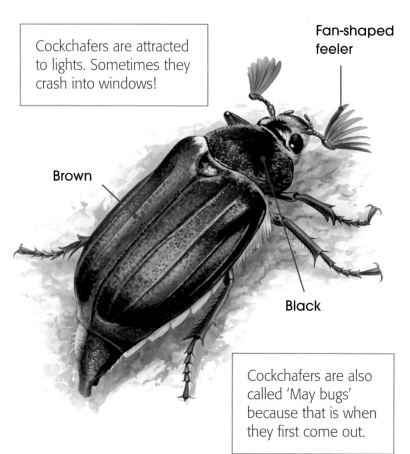

Cockchafers are attracted to lights. Sometimes they crash into windows!

Fan-shaped feeler

Brown

Black

Cockchafers are also called 'May bugs' because that is when they first come out.

Aphid

Aphids are tiny insects. The blackfly and greenfly you see on plants in the garden are types of aphid. This picture is a greenfly. Sometimes aphids can be pink.

Aphids suck the juices from plant stems, leaves and buds.

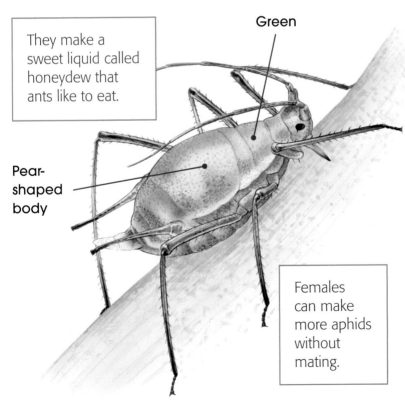

They make a sweet liquid called honeydew that ants like to eat.

Green

Pear-shaped body

Females can make more aphids without mating.

Grasshopper

This is a common field grasshopper.
Look for these in dry, grassy, sunny
places. It comes in different
colours – brown, green, pink,
purple, grey and black!

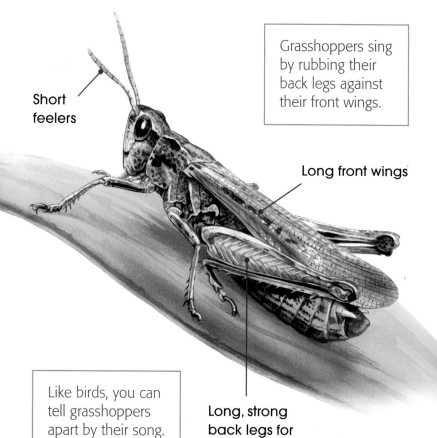

Short
feelers

Grasshoppers sing
by rubbing their
back legs against
their front wings.

Long front wings

Like birds, you can
tell grasshoppers
apart by their song.

Long, strong
back legs for
jumping and singing!

Garden spider

This large spider is also called the cross spider. It has a cross of white spots on its back. It builds a big web to catch insects to eat. Autumn is a good time to see the webs and the spiders.

Watch a spider make a web. They build a new one every day.

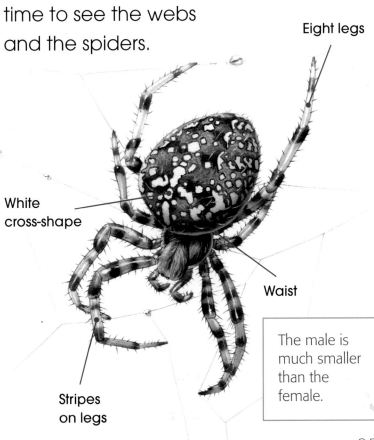

Eight legs

White cross-shape

Waist

The male is much smaller than the female.

Stripes on legs

Woodlouse

Lift up a stone or log in the garden. Watch for woodlice scurrying out. They have seven pairs of legs. Woodlice eat plants and rotting wood.

Female woodlice have little pouches where their eggs grow.

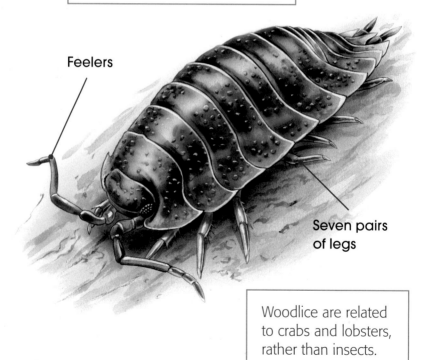

Feelers

Seven pairs of legs

Woodlice are related to crabs and lobsters, rather than insects.

Earthworm

You often see earthworms in the garden. Look for them wriggling about in the soil. They eat dead plants in the earth. Bristles on their belly help them to move.

A 'worm-cast' is a posh way of saying worm poo!

Pointed end is the head end

Saddle – where the eggs are made

An earthworm is male and female at the same time!

Lots of segments.

Bristles – grip soil and help worm move

Put an earthworm on a piece of paper. You can hear its bristles scrape when it moves.

Garden snail

The garden snail is very common. Rainy nights are a good time to look for it. It has a big, round shell. Its body is soft and slimy. It feeds on lots of plants.

A garden snail can seal up its shell to stop it drying out.

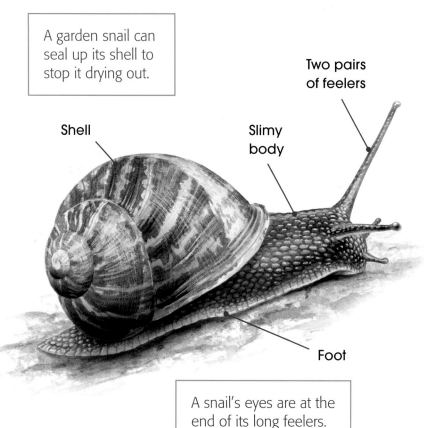

Two pairs of feelers

Shell

Slimy body

Foot

A snail's eyes are at the end of its long feelers.

Banded snail

There are two types of banded snail to look for. To tell them apart look at the 'lip' of the shell. This is the white-lipped banded snail. The other type usually has a very dark 'lip'.

A banded snail's markings help to hide it from hungry birds.

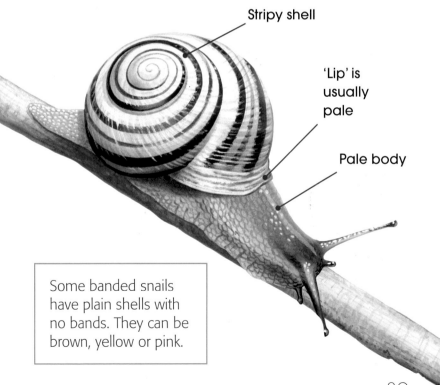

Stripy shell

'Lip' is usually pale

Pale body

Some banded snails have plain shells with no bands. They can be brown, yellow or pink.

 # Slug

Slugs look like snails without the big shell. They are covered in slime which helps them move. This is a garden slug. Slugs can be black, grey, brown or even orange! They eat plants.

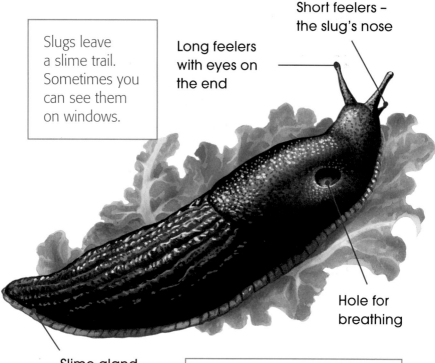

Slugs leave a slime trail. Sometimes you can see them on windows.

Long feelers with eyes on the end

Short feelers – the slug's nose

Hole for breathing

Slime gland

Like snails and earthworms, every slug is male and female.

Useful words

bristles stiff hairs

grubs these are what hatch from
insect eggs

hive where honey bees live

honeydew sweet, sticky plant
juices that aphids give off

maggots the grubs of some flies

nectar the sweet liquid that
flowers make to attract insects

pincers like tweezers on the back
end of an earwig

queen wasp a big female wasp
that lays eggs

Spotter's guide

How many of these
minibeasts have you
seen? Tick them
when you spot them.

☐ Dragonfly
page 6

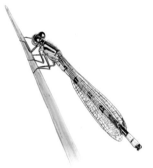

☐ Damselfly
page 7

☐ Bumblebee
page 8

☐ Honeybee
page 9

☐ Wasp
page 10

☐ Ant
page 11

☐ Cinnabar moth
page 12

☐ Garden tiger
moth
page 13

☐ Common blue
butterfly
page 14

☐ Large white
butterfly
page 15

☐ Red admiral
butterfly
page 16

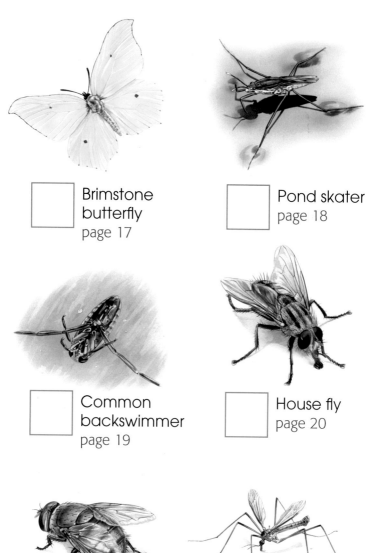

Brimstone
butterfly
page 17

Pond skater
page 18

Common
backswimmer
page 19

House fly
page 20

Bluebottle
page 21

Cranefly
page 22

44

☐ Hoverfly
page 23

☐ Earwig
page 24

☐ Green lacewing
page 25

☐ Mosquito
page 26

☐ Common
froghopper
page 27

☐ Green shield bug
page 28

45

Devil's coach-horse
page 29

Soldier beetle
page 30

Ladybird
page 31

Cockchafer
page 32

Aphid
page 33

Grasshopper
page 34

Garden spider
page 35

Woodlouse
page 36

Earthworm
page 37

Garden snail
page 38

Banded snail
page 39

Slug
page 40

Find out more

If you have enjoyed this book and would like to find out more about minibeasts and other wildlife, you might like RSPB Wildlife Explorers.

Visit www.rspb.org.uk/youth to find lots of things to make and do, and to play brilliant wildlife games.